arco pet handbooks

German Shepherds

Mario Migliorini

New York

The author has been associated with dogs all his life. For the past twenty years Mario Migliorini has earned his living breeding, training, handling, grooming or writing about dogs. He has owned and bred over thirty breeds of his own, and many more for his clients. Among the books he has written or co-authored are *Clipping and Grooming Your Terrier*, *Clipping and Grooming Your Spaniel & Setter*, *Yorkshire Terriers*, *Labrador Retrievers*, *Care and Training Of Your Puppy*, and *Training Your Dog—The Easy Way*.

Third Printing, 1975

Published by ARCO PUBLISHING COMPANY, INC.
219 Park Avenue South, New York, N.Y. 10003

Copyright © Arco Publishing Co., Inc., 1971

Library of Congress Catalog Number 74-126562

ISBN 0-668-03875-6

Printed in the United States of America

CONTENTS

Photo on front cover and above: American and Canadian Champion Vero of Bihari Wonder, CD, CDX, UD, TD, and Canadian CD (the only living dog in the United States who can claim all those titles). Owned by Klaus and Carmen Eifert.

CHAPTER ONE

A PROFILE OF THE BREED

THE GERMAN SHEPHERD has become almost universally known as the "Police Dog" or "German Police Dog." These frequently used misnomers undoubtedly resulted because the breed has been so highly favored by law enforcement agencies both in Germany and throughout the world. A police dog, however, can be any one of several breeds trained to perform the various tasks loosely classified as "police work," including drug detection, tracking or apprehending criminals, and riot control. Each task requires specialized training and a particular dog is usually expected to perform in only one field. For purposes of identification the breed is officially called the "German Shepherd" dog.

New German Shepherd owners should not be misguided by certain preconceived ideas such as the "one-man dog" myth. Everyone likes the idea of owning a one-man dog, but few people realize what a liability such an animal can be. I have only owned one such dog, and I seriously doubt if I would ever burden myself with another one.

A dog that responds only to one person cannot be fed or watered, or cleaned or cared for in any way by anyone but the owner without risk, unless the dog is confined in a special pen. Obviously, a dog cannot be much use as a guard if he has to remain caged all the time. In case of an emergency, a vet may not be able to give treatment without difficulty. In addition, the possibility exists that the dog may get loose and attack someone, even a child. Finally, if the thin bond that holds this dog to its owner is somehow broken, the dog may even attack him. There is no place in our society for such an animal. A *well-trained* security dog is a subtly different matter but even then accidents can occur, and attack-trained dogs definitely do not belong in the home.

King was a beautiful big red and black dog. To me he exemplified all the desirable qualities that a German Shepherd should possess. As a puppy, he appeared to be growing too big to show so his breeder sold him to a well known trainer, who trained him as a free-ranging sentry dog. By virtue of the fact that a "free ranger" works mostly on his own, usually guarding a specific area with little or no supervision, such dogs develop a marked degree of independence and a tendency to act on their own initiative, which can sometimes be a problem.

King belonged to a racetrack. His duties there included discouraging intruders from breaking into the grandstand, and he took his job seriously. No one challenged his authority until one cold winter night when a misguided transient decided that the grandstand would be a good place to sleep. He was wrong! He managed to climb over the seven foot fence, but King spotted him as soon as his feet touched the ground. To save himself, the luckless intruder was forced to climb onto the roof of a small out-building and call for help. The police were called, and soon a nearby prowl car was diverted to the scene. One of the occupants of the car was a rookie cop eager to make his first arrest. As the car slid to a halt he leapt out, gun in hand, ready to apprehend the criminal. In so doing, he got between King and the cornered intruder— that was a mistake! Before the security guard could call off the dog, King had taken hold of the young officer's leg. Fortunately, the dog had worn his fangs down quite short by chewing on the bars of his pen; and as a result he could not do much serious damage. The officer, although badly bruised, suffered more injury to his dignity than to anything else.

Soon after that incident the track installed other security devices and I was able to acquire King, who was still in his prime. He served as my demonstration dog for many years although I had repeated offers to buy him. King was one dog that I could not part with.

Another interesting incident concerned a minister, who was also a well-known broadcaster. His church was located in the south side of Chicago in a particularly tough neighborhood. He was always offering help to anyone who needed it, provided that they visited him at the church. Not only did those in need visit him, but they also robbed him on several occasions when his help had not been as materialistic as they had hoped it would be. As a man of the cloth, the minister hated violence, but he found no joy in being robbed; so he decided that a guard dog would be a good investment.

When the Reverend contacted me, I had only one trained adult available—a big male called Bully. This dog was rather headstrong and still somewhat unruly. He was a good natural guard but had not yet been attack trained, so there was no real reason why he couldn't go into a home. While talking on the telephone to the Minister, I expressed my doubts about the suitability of this particular dog for his purpose. However, as he seemed so anxious to have the dog, I set up an appointment for a demonstration early one morning so that the Reverend could work with the dog under my supervision.

Strangely enough, he never arrived, and I assumed that he had changed his mind; but at eight o'clock that night he arrived with his wife and two teenage children, ready to take the dog home. I brought the dog out and introduced him to the family and he seemed quite at ease with them. So against my better judgment I allowed them to take the dog home that night. I gave them my typed list of instructions and hoped for the best, suggesting that they should call me in case of any problems.

Not unexpectedly, at eight o'clock the next morning the telephone rang and the Reverend informed me, in a very excited voice, that they had had some excitement the night before. It seemed that the minister had been called out on some emergency almost immediately after arriving home. The rest of the family had socialized with the dog for a while before going to bed, leaving him the free run of the house. It was after midnight when the Reverend returned home. Anxious not to disturb the family, he had intended to slip in quietly via the back door; but he had forgotten all about Bully, who refused to let him back into the house. Naturally the resulting din woke everyone up, and the Reverend's wife had to restrain the dog before her husband could enter his own home.

I partly expected to be asked to take the dog back, but when I questioned the minister along this line, he hastily corrected me. "After all," he concluded, "if the dog wouldn't let *me* back into my own home, what possible chance would a burglar have?" To the best of my knowledge the Reverend was never robbed again!

CHAPTER TWO

ORIGIN OF THE GERMAN SHEPHERD

ALTHOUGH THE ORIGIN of the German Shepherd has been linked with *Canis pontiatini,* dating back to the Bronze Age, the breed as we know it has been in existence only since the turn of the century. Its early development is well documented by Rittmeister Max von Stephanitz in his mammoth book *The German Shepherd Dog,* published by the Verein für Deutsche Schäferhunde (SV), The German Shepherd Dog Club of Germany, which Captain von Stephanitz founded in 1899 and dominated for 36 years.

There is little doubt that von Stephanitz successfully controlled the breed's early development. In his book, he describes the heterogeneous mixture of shepherd dogs used to develop the desired characteristics. The Thuringian shepherd provided the erect ears and the wolf-gray color. The Wurttemberg dogs contributed the desired tail carriage and other colors but they also produced "lopped ears." Finally von Stephanitz introduced a big Swabian working dog for its great size, strong back and flowing gait. This crossbreeding produced a marked diversity of type and three different coat varieties.

Through careful inbreeding, rigid controls, and ruthless culling, the Rittmeister directed the task of molding the German Shepherd to his own personal specifications. Later he promoted the use of the German Shepherd as a police and army dog.

In his book, Captain von Stephanitz stressed the adaptability of the breed, and German Shepherds were pictured nursing a variety of orphan animals including lion cubs, puma kits and kittens; tending geese, chickens, calves, hogs, cats, rabbits, fawns, hedgehogs and pigeons; as well as retrieving game, tracking deer and wild boar, catching rats, pulling sleds and carts, herding sheep, guarding children, and leading the blind. Captain von Stephanitz strove to develop a breed that possessed great intelligence and was completely utilitarian.

By 1914, a distinctly homogeneous type had evolved from the original potpourri. At the outbreak of World War I, many Germans donated their dogs for military duty. Incredibly enough, at this time the Geman Shepherd ranked after the Airedale (a British breed), the Boxer, and the Doberman in being accepted. By the end of the war, over 40,000 dogs had been used by the military, a high percentage of which were German Shepherds.

After the war, many "captured" German Shepherds found their way from Germany to the United States and Britain. Two Englishmen, Lt. Col. Moore-Brabazon and Lt. Col. Baldwin, were responsible for taking a number of good specimens back to Britain, where the breed was renamed "Alsatian Wolfdog," probably because some of these dogs came from the Alsace Lorraine district of France where they were known as "Chien Loup." The name "Wolfdog" was dropped in 1930, and in Britain the breed has been known as the Alsatian since that time.

Two dogs were destined to influence the popularity of the breed unlike any other dogs have ever done. These two were the famous movie dogs, Strongheart and Rin Tin Tin, and their exploits on the silver screen created a worldwide demand for German Shepherds. While this demand soared, puppy mills turned out an estimated 25,000 puppies a year in the United States alone. As a result of much indiscriminate breeding, the quality of the breed declined sharply, and only the combined efforts of the German Shepherd Dog Club of

America and many sincere and dedicated breeders prevented its complete degeneration.

In 1922, the German Shepherd Dog Club of Germany introduced a system of grading individuals (Ankorung). Not only did the S.V. endorse or discourage certain matings, but they even banned breeding from dogs that in their opinion might produce undesirable characteristics. Many of these rejected specimens found their way to the United States. One of these was Nores von der Kriminalpolizei, the sire of Strongheart, who was used extensively by those wishing to cash in on the name of his famous offspring.

Meanwhile, Mrs. Harrison Eustes, with the help of Willi Ebeleng and Elliot Humphrey, was conducting extensive breeding experiments in Switzerland in an attempt to develop a superior strain of German Shepherd. They eventually founded The Seeing Eye Guide Dog School at Morristown, New Jersey, using dogs originating from this highly selective breeding program.

By 1940, the Germans had trained an estimated 20,000 dogs for military use. At the outbreak of World War II, the United States had no trained war dogs, and it was a civilian group, called Dogs for Defense Inc., that started to recruit dogs for use by the Armed Services.

The German Shepherd became the official U.S. Navy and Coast Guard dog, partly through the efforts of individuals like John Gaus. A total of some 10,000 dogs were used during the war. Later, the U.S. Air Force established a program to train dogs to guard its bases and installations throughout the world. At the present time German Shepherds are widely used by all branches of the military, both in war zones and at home, almost to the exclusion of all other breeds. Anyone wishing to donate a dog for such work should write to Military Working Dogs, Det 37 (SAAMA), Lackland AFB, Texas 78236.

CHAPTER THREE

THE STANDARD

BEING REGISTERED BY the American Kennel Club is only a part of the requirements for a show dog. The dog must also qualify as a representative of its breed by conforming to the A.K.C. Standard, which has been adopted for the breed. Included in the Standard are specifications which, if not complied with, incur mandatory disqualification from A.K.C. competition. For example, all males that are either monorchid or cryptorchid (have only one, or no testicles in the scrotum) are automatically disqualified.

The official American Kennel Club Standard* for the German Shepherd is as follows:

GERMAN SHEPHERD DOG

GENERAL APPEARANCE. The first impression of a good German Shepherd Dog is that of a strong, agile, well-muscled animal, alert and full of life. It is well balanced, with harmonious development of the forequarter and hindquarter. The dog is longer than tall, deep-bodied, and presents an outline of smooth curves rather than angles. It looks substantial and not spindly, giving the impression, both at rest and in motion, of muscular fitness and nimbleness without any look

---

* Reprinted by permission of the American Kennel Club.

of clumsiness or soft living. The ideal dog is stamped with a look of quality and nobility—difficult to define, but unmistakable when present. Secondary sex characteristics are strongly marked, and every animal gives a definite impression of masculinity or femininity, according to its sex.

CHARACTER. The breed has a distinct personality marked by direct and fearless, but not hostile, expression, self-confidence and a certain aloofness that does not lend itself to immediate and indiscriminate friendships. The dog must be approachable, quietly standing its ground and showing confidence and willingness to meet overtures without itself making them. It is poised, but when the occasion demands, eager and alert; both fit and willing to serve in its capacity as companion, watchdog, blind leader, herding dog, or guardian, whichever the circumstances may demand. The dog must not be timid, shrinking behind its master or handler; it should not be nervous, looking about or upward with anxious expression or showing nervous reactions, such as tucking of tail, to strange sounds or sights. Lack of confidence under any surroundings is not typical of good character. Any of the above deficiencies in character which indicate shyness must be penalized as very serious faults. It must be possible for the judge to observe the teeth and to determine that both testicles are descended. Any dog that attempts to bite the judge must be disqualified. The ideal dog is a working animal with an incorruptible character combined with body and gait suitable for the arduous work that constitutes its primary purpose.

HEAD. The head is noble, cleanly chiseled, strong without coarseness, but above all not fine, and in proportion to the body. The head of the male is distinctly masculine, and that of the bitch distinctly feminine. The muzzle is long and strong with the lips firmly fitted, and its topline is parallel to the topline of the skull. Seen from the front, the forehead is only moderately arched, and the skull slopes into the long, wedge-shaped muzzle without abrupt stop. Jaws are strongly developed. *Ears*— Ears are moderately pointed, in proportion to the skull, open toward the front, and carried erect when at attention, the ideal carriage being one in which the center lines of the ears, viewed from the front, are parallel to each other and perpendicular to the ground. A dog with cropped or hanging ears must be disqualified. *Eyes*—of medium size, almond shaped, set a little obliquely and not protruding. The color is as dark as possible. The expression keen, intelligent and composed. *Teeth*—42 in number—20 upper and 22 lower—are strongly developed and meet in a scissors bite in which part of the inner surface of the upper incisors meet and engage part of the outer surface of the lower incisors. An overshot jaw or a level bite is undesirable. An undershot jaw is a disqualifying fault. Complete dentition is to be preferred. Any missing teeth other than first premolars is a serious fault.

NECK. The neck is strong and muscular, clean-cut and relatively long, proportionate in size to the head and without loose folds of skin. When the dog is at attention or excited, the head is raised and the neck carried high; otherwise typical carriage of the head is forward rather than up and but little higher than the top of the shoulders, particularly in motion.

FOREQUARTERS. The shoulder blades are long and obliquely angled, laid on flat and not placed forward. The upper arm joins the shoulder blade at about a right angle. Both the upper arm and the shoulder blade are well muscled. The forelegs, viewed from all sides, are straight and the bone oval rather than round. The pasterns are strong and springy and angulated at approximately a 25-degree angle from the vertical.

FEET. The feet are short, compact, with toes well arched, pads thick and firm, nails short and dark. The dewclaws, if any, should be removed from the hind legs. Dewclaws on the forelegs may be removed, but are normally left on.

PROPORTION. The German Shepherd Dog is longer than tall, with the most desirable proportion as 10 to 8½. The desired height for males at the top of the highest point of the shoulder blade is 24 to 26 inches; and for bitches, 22 to 24 inches. The length is measured from the point of the prosternum or breast bone to the rear edge of the pelvis, the ischial tuberosity.

BODY. The whole structure of the body gives an impression of depth and solidity without bulkiness. *Chest*—Commencing at the prosternum, it is well filled and carried well down between the legs. It is deep and capacious, never shallow, with ample room for lungs and heart, carried well forward, with the prosternum showing ahead of the shoulder in profile. *Ribs*—Well sprung and long, neither barrel-shaped nor too flat, and carried down to a sternum which reaches to the elbows. Correct ribbing allows the elbows to move back freely when the dog is at a trot. Too round causes interference and throws the elbows out; too flat or short causes pinched elbows. Ribbing is carried well back so that the loin is relatively short. *Abdomen*—Firmly held and not paunchy. The bottom line is only moderately tucked up in the loin.

TOPLINE. *Withers*—The withers are higher than and sloping into the level back. *Back*—The back is straight, very strongly developed without sag or roach, and relatively short. The desirable long proportion is not derived from a long back, but from over-all length with relation to height, which is achieved by length of forequarter and length of withers and hindquarter, viewed from the side. *Loin*—Viewed from the top, broad and strong. Undue length between the last rib and the thigh, when viewed from the side, is undesirable. *Croup*— Long and gradually sloping. *Tail*—Bushy, with the last vertebra extended at least to the hock joint. It is set smoothly into the croup and low rather than high. At rest, the tail hangs in a slight curve like a saber. A slight hook—sometimes carried to one side—is faulty only to the extent that it mars general appearance. When the dog is excited or in motion, the curve is accentuated and the tail raised, but it should never be curled forward beyond a vertical line. Tails too short, or with clumpy ends due to ankylosis, are serious faults. A dog with a docked tail must be disqualified.

HINDQUARTERS. The whole assembly of the thigh, viewed from the side, is broad, with both upper and lower thigh well muscled, forming as nearly as possible a right angle. The upper thigh bone parallels the shoulder blade while the lower thigh bone parallels the upper arm. The metatarsus (the unit between the hock joint and the foot) is short, strong and tightly articulated.

GAIT. A German Shepherd Dog is a trotting dog, and its structure has been developed to meet the requirements of its work. *General Impression*—The gait is outreaching, elastic, seemingly without effort, smooth and rhythmic, covering the maximum amount of ground with the minimum number of steps. At a walk it covers a great deal of ground, with long stride of both hind legs and forelegs. At a trot the dog covers still more ground with even longer stride, and moves powerfully but easily, with co-ordination and balance so that the gait appears to be the steady motion of a well-lubricated machine. The feet travel close to the ground on both forward reach and backward push. In order to achieve ideal movement of this kind, there must be good muscular development and ligamentation. The hindquarters deliver, through the back, a powerful forward thrust which slightly lifts the whole animal and drives the body forward. Reaching far under, and passing the imprint left by the front foot, the hind foot takes hold of the ground; then hock, stifle and upper thigh come into play and sweep back, the stroke of the hind leg finishing with the foot still close to the ground in a smooth follow-through. The over-reach of the hindquarter usually necessitates one hind foot passing outside and the other hind foot passing inside the track of the forefeet, and such action is not faulty unless the locomotion is crabwise with the dog's body sideways out of the normal straight line.

TRANSMISSION. The typical smooth, flowing gait is maintained with great strength and firmness of back. The whole effort of the hindquarter is transmitted to the forequarter through the loin, back and withers. At full trot, the back must remain firm and level without sway, roll, whip or roach. Unlevel topline with withers lower than the hip is a fault. To compensate for the forward motion imparted by the hindquarters, the shoulder should open to its full extent. The forelegs should reach out close to the ground in a long stride in harmony with that of the hindquarters. The dog does not track on widely separated parallel lines, but brings the feet inward toward the middle line of the body when trotting in order to maintain balance. The feet track closely but do not strike or cross over. Viewed from the front, the front legs function from the shoulder joint to the pad in a straight line. Viewed rom the rear, the hind legs function from the hip joint to the pad in a straight line. Faults of gait, whether from front, rear or side, are to be considered very serious faults.

COLOR. The German Shepherd Dog varies in color, and most colors are permissible. Strong rich colors are preferred. Nose black. Pale, washed-out colors and blues or livers are serious faults. A white dog or a dog with a nose that is not predominantly black, must be disqualified.

COAT. The ideal dog has a double coat of medium length. The outer coat should be as dense as possible, hair straight, harsh and lying close to the body. A slightly wavy outer coat, often of wiry texture, is permissible. The head, including the inner ear and foreface, and the legs and paws are covered with short hair, and the neck with longer and thicker hair. The rear of the forelegs and hind legs has somewhat longer hair extending to the pastern and hock, respectively. Faults in coat include soft, silky, too long outer coat, woolly, curly, and open coat.

DISQUALIFICATIONS

Cropped or hanging ears. Undershot jaw. Docked tail. White dogs. Dogs with noses not predominantly black. Any dog that attempts to bite the judge.

Approved April 9, 1968

To the novice, the Standard may appear to make overwhelming demands of perfection that would certainly eliminate a high percentage of German Shepherds as show specimens. In order to enable you to make some assessment as to the quality of your own prospect, it is advisable to attend a number of dog shows. Pay particular attention to the winners, especially of the Best of Breed class. Don't be afraid to consult experts along the way.

Two typical, alert German Shepherd puppies. Note the position of the ears, which usually are not fully erect until the puppies have finished teething.

Puppies love to romp and play.

A fine profile view of a mature German Shepherd.

Any boy would be proud to own a German Shepherd puppy.

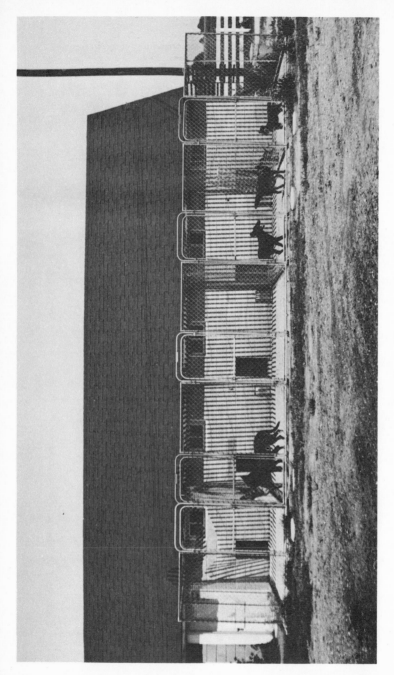

Ideal German Shepherd kenneling facilities.

CHAPTER FOUR

BUYING A PUPPY

IF YOU ARE interested in buying a puppy, go to a reputable breeder—that is, a person who has established a reputation for breeding and selling quality specimens and who honors the Breeder's Code set down by the German Shepherd Dog Club of America. While the initial cost might be slightly higher through him, and although price alone is no criterion for quality, the deal may well prove to be cheaper in the long run.

Ask to see the parents, or at least the dam, of any puppy that you are considering. If she is a poor representative of the breed, it is unlikely that her puppies will be outstanding. Regardless of the quality of the sire, if she has major faults and poor conformation, it is quite possible that her offspring will be likewise. State frankly what you want. If you hope to show your puppy, say so, and do not be too ready to reject the experienced breeder's opinion in favor of your own in this respect.

If you are permitted to choose from a litter, select an active puppy. Look for a straight back, straight legs, good feet, ample bone, and a shiny flat coat. The tail should be long and wagging and the eyes dark and bright. Young puppies should be friendly and uninhibited. Avoid quiet, shy individuals. Examine the mouth carefully. If the puppy's teeth are not yet fully developed, pay close attention to the gums. If the lower gums protrude noticeably beyond the upper, there is a good possibility that the puppy might develop an undershot jaw. If the upper gums protrude, the jaw may become overshot.

Above all, choose a puppy that you like. There is no guarantee of how any puppy will eventually turn out, so it is always a good idea to pick one that you are going to enjoy. While the show aspect and all that it means may be important, there is another equally important consideration in the purchase—that of finding a friend and companion. In this respect, it hardly matters if the puppy develops into a show specimen or not. He can still be a keen, alert, observant pal and every bit as much fun as any show dog, perhaps more. For that reason, your puppy should always receive, from the beginning, the utmost care and attention.

When the sale has been finalized, you should receive either a blue A.K.C. Registration Application form, or a white and purple A.K.C. Registration Certificate, filled out on the back and signed over to you by the previous owner. This will enable you to transfer the registration to your own name. You should also receive a copy of at least a three-generation pedigree.

The A.K.C. recommends that if the seller cannot give you the registration application, you should demand and receive an identification of your dog, consisting of the breed, the registered name and number of your dog's sire and dam, and its date of birth. If the litter of which your dog is a part has been recorded with the A.K.C., then the litter registration number is sufficient identification.

Don't be misled by promises of "paper" later, but demand a registration form or proper identification. If neither is supplied, don't buy the dog.

For more details, send for a pamphlet on the subject to the American Kennel Club, Dept. Y, 51 Madison Avenue, New York, N.Y. 10010.

CHAPTER FIVE

PUPPY FEEDING SCHEDULE

As soon as a new puppy arrives in the home, he must be put on a strict feeding schedule. Evaporated milk, diluted with half water, is a recommended substitute for cow's milk to reduce the risk of diarrhea. Food should always be given at room temperature.

1st	Feed	PABLUM, made with evaporated milk
2nd	Feed	SPECIALIZED PET DIET #2 (Puppy Diet)
3rd	Feed	SPECIALIZED PET DIET plus milk
4th	Feed	SPECIALIZED PET DIET plus milk
5th	Feed	PABLUM

For young puppies, add a small quantity of evaporated milk to the Puppy Diet and mash with a fork until it has a nice creamy consistency. Other brands may be used in place of those recommended here. Baby and Junior foods, although expensive, make good substitutes for very small puppies. Avitron drops and Theralin should be added according to the directions on the label.

Give puppies six to eight weeks of age five meals daily. At eight weeks of age, eliminate the third feed. At twelve weeks of age, discontinue Pablum, and just feed the puppy three regular meals. Milk may be discontinued, at the owner's discretion.

The average total daily requirements should be divided into appropriate portions:

Size	Dry Food	Canned Food
Toy Breeds	⅓ cup	⅓ can
Small	2 cups	1½ cans
Medium	3 cups	2 cans
Large	4 cups	2½ cans
Giant	5 cups	3 cans

Although drinking water should be made available at all times, some puppies will drink too much at one time, while others will simply spill most of it. If your puppy happens to be one of the latter, small drinks of water should be given regularly between meals.

CHAPTER SIX

WORMING

THE WORM PROBLEM is more complex than is generally realized. There are four types of worms that the new dog owner should know about: Roundworms, Tapeworms, Hookworms and Whipworms. These parasites can infest both young puppies and old dogs during any period of their lives, including prenatally, if the mother is infected. There is a widespread belief that the presence of worms can be detected by watching for them to appear in the stool, which is partially correct. A severe infestation of Roundworms or Tapeworms can result in adult Roundworms, or Tapeworm segments, being passed occasionally.

However, the absence of such signs does not conclusively eliminate the possibility of an infection. "Hooks" and "Whips," which attach themselves to the lining of the intestines, are rarely passed, and even more rarely seen. Whipworms are about two inches long, shaped like a stock whip; one third of the length representing the body, the remaining two thirds the thread-like tail. Hookworms are little more than half an inch in length and resemble an exaggerated letter "C."

The only reliable method of diagnosing the presence of these debilitating parasites is by microscopic examination of a fresh stool specimen. This is a job for an experienced technician, and involves the use of costly laboratory equipment. Although there are worming preparations readily available to everyone, each species requires specific treatment for the best results; i.e., Piperazine for Roundworms, Nemural for Tapes, D.N.P. for Hooks and Whipside for Worms, just to name a few of the available medicines.

As you are unlikely to be able to determine if your dog has worms without professional advice, consult your veterinarian on the subject, for he is qualified to help you.

CHAPTER SEVEN

INFECTIOUS DISEASES

CANINE VIRUS DISTEMPER, an air-borne infection, is a very serious contagious disease. The mortality rate, especially among puppies and unimmunized victims, is extremely high. Initial indication may be a high fever lasting for several days, which then suddenly returns to normal. This is followed by loss of appetite and bloody diarrhea, which in turn causes dehydration. Runny eyes and nose, coughing, sneezing, catarrh, gagging, and respiratory infection are symptomatic of the disease, which affects almost every organ in the body.

HARDPAD, considered by many as a secondary infection, frequently coincides with distemper. It is characterized by hardening of the pads of the feet. The virus eventually attacks the central nervous system causing encephalitis. Convulsions, stiffening of the body and chewing fits usually occur. Dogs recovering from hardpad disease are invariably left with some degree of chorea, in addition to other side effects. Although puppies should receive some degree of temporary immunity from the mother, this fact cannot be relied on. A blood test to determine what degree of immunity puppies have was developed at Cornell University. To have any practical applications, however, this test should be made before the puppies are sold.

Although there are certain times of the year when distemper and hardpad appear to be more prevalent than others, waiting to get protection is not advisable. Symptoms occur six to nine days after infection, and usually prognosis is unfavorable.

INFECTIOUS HEPATITIS affects many areas of the body, especially the liver. Virus is present in all secretions during the infectious stages. Symptoms range from moderate to severe, sometimes leading to complications such as total or partial paralysis, excessive bleeding, anemia and tonsillitis. Abdominal discomfort, watery eyes, listlessness, loss of appetite, rapid breathing, intensive thirst, vomiting, trembling and fluctuating temperature are all indicative of hepatitis. Virus in the urine of animals which have recovered from the disease is considered a major source of infection. The incubation period is six to nine days. Treatment may include antibiotics and blood transfusions. It has been estimated that a high percentage of all dogs contract some degree of this disease, making spontaneous recovery without the owners realizing that the animal has been sick. This disease also occurs in conjunction with distemper.

LEPTOSPIROSIS is spread by contact with an infected animal, dog or rat, through bacteria in the urine. Symptoms appear suddenly. Weakness, lack of appetite, fever followed by a subnormal temperature, stiffness and reluctance to stand, bleeding gums, frequent urination, bloody diarrhea and general debilitation occur. Puppy losses are usually high.

If your puppy has not had any shots at all, it is advisable to discuss the matter with your veterinarian, who will be happy to advise you about the various procedures.

RABIES is an infectious disease that can affect all mammals. The virus is usually transmitted in the saliva of infected animals as the result of a bite or by the contamination of an open wound. Contact of the saliva with unbroken skin does not result in infection. Prolonged confinement with infected animals was recently proven to be another possible method of transmitting infection.

Inflammation of the brain and spinal cord affects the central nervous system and death invariably occurs. The time lapse between infection and the onset of encephalitis varies with the site of contamination. The nearer to the brain it is, the more rapidly symptoms develop. Rabies symptoms, which can be both vague and misleading, are rarely as dramatic as is generally supposed. Affected animals may just stop eating or drinking, or seek seclusion. Abrupt personality changes may also occur. Other symptoms, equally related to less serious conditions, may also exist. Outbreaks of rabies in the U.S.A. have been reduced by considerably more than half over the past twenty years. 3,591 incidents were recorded nationally in 1968. 542 cases involved domestic animals, of which 295 were dogs. Uncontrolled strays are often a contributing factor in such incidents. Figures for 1969 indicate a slight reduction. 101 fewer incidents were reported nationally, domestic animals accounting for 57 of them.

Vaccinating both dogs and cats against the disease is a sound precaution. Unless you have ample reason to believe that your pet has been in contact with a rabid animal, there is no cause for anxiety.

Dogs suspected of rabies should not be destroyed, but rather taken to a veterinarian for observation and testing.

It has been estimated that only a small percentage of all humans exposed to the virus are ever affected. Anyone who is bitten by a rabid animal can be successfully treated, prior to the onset of symptoms, by the Pasteur treatment. This method of aborting rabies stimulates production of antibodies through successive injections with virus of gradually increasing strength over a period of fourteen days. A new single injection method is currently being tested.

CHAPTER EIGHT

COMMON PARASITES

TICKS. There are several hundred species of ticks, although only two, the brown dog tick, and a variety of wood tick known as the American dog tick, are of importance to the dog owner. Of these, the American dog tick is the most dangerous, being the principal carrier of Rocky Mountain Spotted Fever, along with the Rocky Mountain Spotted Fever tick which only occurs in the region for which it was named.

Without going too deeply into the life cycle of the parasite, it is worth mentioning that, depending on the species, each female may produce anywhere from 2,000 to 6,000 eggs. Having a three host cycle, the parasite must have a meal of blood before it can develop from one stage to another, but may survive long periods of time between hosts. Unfed larvas have been known to survive for 540 days, nymphs for 584 days, and adults for more than four years. This creates obvious problems in the event of an infestation, and the appearance of ticks on your dog should not be treated lightly.

To remove a single tick, attach a pair of forceps or tweezers over the site where the tick's head is buried, as close to the dog's skin as possible, wait for a few moments and withdraw the tick and dispose of it. Ticks should not be handled with bare hands.

In the event of an infestation, the dog must be dipped in a special solution. A suitable emergency solution can be made with 51% Malathion, available at most garden centers, using

2¼ tablespoons to one gallon of water. Soak the dog with this solution, allow to stand for five minutes and towel dry. Take special care that none of the solution goes into the dog's eyes. The premises may be sprayed with the same product, using ten tablespoons to one gallon of water. Sevin dust may also be used, as directed on the label. Lambert-Kay's "Victory Flea Collar" and "Flea Shield" aerosol spray are two products recommended as effective in controlling external parasites.

FLEAS. Parasites have no redeeming features, especially the flea, whose only function is to create discomfort. Strangely enough, its presence is often accepted as the inevitable consequence of owning a pet, which is unfortunate. Fleas are frequently found on both wild and domestic animals such as dogs, cats, rats, raccoons, foxes, rabbits, and even on man.

In addition to being a voracious feeder, the flea acts as intermediary host to other parasites, such as tapeworm, roundworm, and possibly heartworm.

While a severe infestation might cause anemia, even a single flea is capable of creating parasitical dermatosis, due to an irritant in its saliva which may in turn produce other allergic reactions.

The peak infestation period seems to occur around July and August, perhaps a little earlier or later depending on the region in which you live.

Fleas generally respond to the same treatment as indicated for ticks.

MOSQUITOS & HEARTWORM. The most important feature about the mosquito from the dog owner's point of view, in addition to the personal discomfort created, is the fact that this objectionable parasite also acts as the intermediary host for the heartworm. The highest incidence of heartworm infection is reported in areas where salt-marsh mosquitos are most abundant. The vector ingests the microfilariae while feeding on an infected animal. After a period of ten to fourteen days the microfilariae develop into larvae within the mosquito, and are subsequently injected into another host as the insect feeds. The larvae develop in the subcutaneous and muscular connective tissues, where they grow to approximately one to four inches in length, and subsequently migrate to the right ventrical by way of the veins to continue their development. After about eight months, these worms become adult, reaching up to twelve inches in length, and start releasing microfilariae which immediately begin to circulate in the bloodstream.

For those who may be concerned by the presence of mosquitos in their area, and afraid that their dogs may have been exposed to heartworm infection, the most common clinical symptom is a chronic cough and lack of stamina. Little is known about the life of the adult worm, but it has been suggested that the life expectancy of the parasite may exceed five years or more. It is also considered unlikely that any immunity to infection is ever developed.

Heartworm treatment takes two forms: Microfilaricides such as Dizan (oral) and Talodex (injectible); or Adulticides, which are arsenical drugs. As the adult worm is the major cause of debilitation, the initial procedure is to treat the adult infection, followed in a number of weeks by treatment to remove the microfilariae from the system.

A preventative course of treatment consisting of periodic injections of Talodex, starting at four months of age, designed to control the development of larvae and microfilariae within the dog, is being introduced; but positive conclusions as to its success appear premature at this point. A similar system, using Dizan tablets twice annually for a period of several days, seems to have received more general acceptance among veterinarians.

The presence of heartworm is diagnosed by taking a blood sample from the dog and examining it under a microscope to determine the presence of microfilariae. Naturally, this is also a job for your veterinarian.

CHAPTER NINE

TRAINING

LEASH TRAINING. Leash breaking the puppy is quite a simple matter when done correctly. Never attempt to train him in the house, or even in the backyard, as this will interfere with the security of his home, causing confusion and possible resentment.

Begin by carrying the puppy, wearing his collar and leash, about 100 yards from your home. Place the puppy on the ground at your feet, then, giving him a reassuring pat and a few words of encouragement, walk briskly away from the puppy, as if you were going to abandon him. Hold the leash loosely in your right hand and do not make any attempt to drag the puppy. Nine times out of ten, he will panic at the thought of being left alone in unfamiliar surroundings and will quickly follow you home. If he hesitates, give him a light jerk on the leash while encouraging him to come towards you. By using the puppy's natural fear of being left alone in a strange place, you are forcing him to seek the refuge of your company, making him totally reliant on you for his security. If you leave, it is only natural that he will quickly follow.

Once the puppy is walking nicely on the leash, start walking past your home before turning back and going in. Do this until the puppy follows freely wherever you go. Don't wait too long before starting to leash train your puppy. If he is old enough to walk, he is old enough to train. Make each lesson short, of never more than five minutes' duration at a time.

A simple nylon slip collar, commonly called a choke collar, is by far the most humane type of training collar for a young puppy, although a chain is sometimes preferable for training adult dogs. Contrary to what the name implies, a choke collar does not actually choke the dog at all, but merely constricts the neck, causing the dog to instinctively contract his neck muscles against the pressure. Subsequently, a light jerk on the leash is less apt to injure the puppy than a similar jerk on a regular collar, which could cause jarring damage to the windpipe. Another significant feature of this device is that it is virtually impossible for a dog to slip out of it, making it safe to take the puppy out onto the highway.

HOUSEBREAKING. It is extremely easy to house train a puppy with newspapers. Start with several sheets close to the puppy's bed. Apply one drop of "Good Boy Housebreaking Aid" in the center of each sheet. Gradually move the paper towards the door, reducing the number of sheets until you are using only one or two sheets. Finally, take the puppy outside to the area of your choice. Apply several drops of Housebreaking Aid to this area and encourage the puppy to use it. Remain with him until he does, then praise him. Never shut a small puppy outside on his own during this period of training, as the isolation will only make him so worried and insecure that he may completely forget to relieve himself until he gets back into the house.

CRATE TRAINING. This type of training is useful for those planning to travel with their dog, whether going to dog shows or simply while on vacation. It is always a good idea to have your German Shepherd accustomed to being crated. While there are several good reasons for doing this, possibly the most important one is for his own safety.

Contrary to what the novice may feel about confining his pet in a small cage or box, most dogs like having their own crate to hide away in. If it is left on the floor with the door open, they will often sleep in it, in preference to anywhere else. The crate also offers a sense of security when your pet is taken to a strange place, such as a motel, and a greater degree of safety in a moving vehicle.

Start confining the puppy to his crate for a short period of time every day, ideally after the puppy has been playing and is ready for sleep. Initially, he may cry for a little while, but that will soon wear off, and in no time at all, your puppy will go into his crate quite happily.

Once the puppy is quite secure in his crate, put the crate in your vehicle and let the puppy stay there for about an hour every day for a week or so. Then, when he appears to have settled down, take him for a short drive. By using this method, you can expect to make your dog a seasoned traveler in no time at all.

THE GERMAN SHEPHERD IN OBEDIENCE. As a breed, the German Shepherd rates high among the ranks of obedience award winners. They are usually keen enthusiastic workers, easy to train and delightful to watch.

All dogs should learn "basic obedience." This training opens up an important means of communication between a dog and its owner.

Learning immediate response to such commands as "Heel," "Come," "Sit," "Down," and "Stay" should form an essential part of each dog's formal training.

To become an Obedience Champion, a dog must obtain three qualifying scores of at least 170 points (out of a possible 200) under three different judges, scoring not less than 50% of the points allowed for each exercise. This must be done at three A.K.C. licensed, or member obedience trials, with an entry of six or more at each trial.

The following chart indicates the approximate amount of food intake required for optimum good health. Extreme cold, increased activity or physiological stress could increase this requirement by as much as 200%. Needless to say, as dogs grow older and less active, these needs also decline.

OBEDIENCE EXERCISES

Novice exercises, for the title Companion Dog and the right to use the letters C.D. after the dog's name:

1.	Heel on Leash	35 points
2.	Stand for Examination	30 points
3.	Heel Free	45 points
4.	Recall	30 points
5.	Long Sit	30 points
6.	Long Down	30 points
	Maximum Total Score	200 points

Open Class exercises, for the title Companion Dog Excellent (C.D.X):

1.	Heel Free	40 points
2.	Drop on Recall	30 points
3.	Retrieve on Flat	25 points
4.	Retrieve over High Jump	35 points
5.	Broad Jump	20 points
6.	Long Sit	25 points
7.	Long Down	25 points
	Maximum Total Score	200 points

Utility exercises for the title Utility Dog (U.D.):

1.	Scent Discrimination— Article No. 1	30 points
2.	Scent Discrimination— Article No. 2	30 points
3.	Directed Retrieve	30 points
4.	Signal Exercise	35 points
5.	Directed Jumping	40 points
6.	Group Examination	35 points
	Maximum Total Score	200 points

The American Kennel Club will issue a Tracking Dog certificate to a registered dog, and will permit the use of the
letters "T.D." after the name of each dog which has been
certified by the two judges to have passed a licensed, or member tracking test in which at least three dogs actually
competed.

The owner of a dog holding both the U.D. and T.D. titles
may use the letters "U.D.T." after the name of the dog, sig-
nifying "Utility Dog Tracker."

The owner of a dog holding a U.D.T. degree can be justly
proud of his achievement. In order to be able to train your
dog well enough to compete in obedience trials, it is advisable
to join your local Obedience Training Club.

*A well-schooled German Shepherd dog is a joy to own. This obe-
dient group belongs to the Delaware State Police Department.*

The well-trained police dog will not let anything stand in the way of apprehending a suspect. Constant training keeps him ready for any eventuality.

Dogs are trained to attack by developing their inherent protective instincts. Attack-trained animals can be a liability to their owners and do not belong in the home.

Tracker dogs are not only trained to track down criminals but also to locate persons lost in wilderness areas. The lives of many lost children have been saved by these canine specialists.

CHAPTER TEN

FEEDING AND EXERCISE

THE GERMAN SHEPHERD is a strong, hardy dog and doesn't require pampering. Good food and exercise are two of the most important contributions to his continued good health.

Controlled exercise, in the form of daily road work, is undoubtedly the best conditioning exercise for any breed of dog. Walking will rapidly improve muscle tone, tighten up the feet, and wear down the nails. If possible, walk your dog several blocks every day. After a while, you may even find yourself in better condition.

FEEDING REQUIREMENTS. In addition to an unspecified amount of carbohydrate, dog food should contain not less than 15% fat and 20% protein, together with the correct balance of the following vitamins and minerals which are essential for maintaining a normal healthy animal. Vitamins: A, D, E, K, B12, Thiamine, Riboflavin, Pyridoxine, Pantothenic Acid, Niacin, Choline and Ascorbic Acid. Minerals: Calcium, Phosphorus, Iron, Copper, Potassium, Iodine, Magnesium, Sodium, Manganese, Cobalt and Zinc.

Commercial dog food companies concentrate heavily on owner-appeal. Numerous ads draw a positive resemblance between certain products and the food that you might put on your own table, such as beef or hamburger, thus making it appear more appetizing. That "good red meat" look can be created by the addition of nitrate. Convenience is also a strong selling point; but unless you are willing to accept *some* degree of inconvenience, you shouldn't have a dog in the first place!

Based on considerable experience, it is my conclusion that a high percentage of young dogs are undernourished. This does not necessarily mean that they are *underfed,* although it is highly probable.

NUTRITIONAL REQUIREMENT CHART

Based on a study by the National Research Council

Weight of Dog	*Dry Dog Food*		*Canned Dog Food*	
LBS.	*Average Daily Requirement per dog in LBS.*		*Average Daily Requirement per dog in CANS*	
	ADULT	PUPPY	ADULT	PUPPY
5	3 oz.	6 oz.	½	1
10	5 oz.	10 oz.	1	2
15	6 oz.	12 oz.	1¼	2½
20	8 oz.	1 lb. 16 oz.	1½	3
30	12 oz.	1 lb. 8 oz.	2¼	4½
50	1 lb. 4 oz.	2 lb. 8 oz.	3½	7
70	1 lb. 12 oz.	3 lb. 4 oz.	5	10
110	2 lb. 12 oz.	—	8	—

Doubling the fat content of dry dog food should reduce the above requirements by some 10%. However, increases beyond that amount might limit the intake enough to create a diet imbalance—a common feature where household table-scraps are over-abundant. In sharp contrast, canned dog foods would require the addition of 100% fat to achieve a similar result, due to a much greater moisture content—often as much as 70% moisture.

NUTRITIONAL SUPPLEMENTS. Dog food manufacturers invariably claim that their products are completely nutritious and that no additional supplements are required. Even so, under specific stress conditions, the need for certain vitamins and minerals increases dramatically. Stress factors are usually present during the growing and teething stages, during pregnancy, lactation, following surgery or sickness, as well as during periods of increased activity such as hunting. This suggests the need to supplement the regular commercial diet at least intermittently. This also applies to the poor eater, for the impressive analysis printed on the package is only significant if the dog consumes the contents.

FAT. Most dry dog food products are high in carbohydrates but low in fat, possibly to retard spoilage. The addition of lard or bacon fat will correct this deficiency. Daily amounts should range from a teaspoonful for toys or small puppies, to two or three tablespoonsful for the giant breeds. Fat yields the most energy and aids in producing a good coat and healthy skin. Experiments have also shown that dogs given ample fat are less excitable and have better temperaments than those on a low fat diet.

VITAMIN A. Vitamin A is essential for good eyesight and healthy skin, and is also needed for the absorption of fat. Dandruff is one significant sign of vitamin A deficiency. Another might be swollen joints, unthriftiness, low fertility, and poor resistance to disease.

VITAMIN B COMPLEX. B Vitamins are essential for combating anemia, i.e., following a severe parasitic infection. Excessive loss of hair, skin fungus, dermatitis and itching, nervousness, constipation, loss of weight, listlessness, conjunctivitis, corneal opacities, and poor appetite are also symptomatic of this deficiency. A simple indication is constant scratching and chewing of the feet. Brewer's yeast and liver extracts are the most readily available source of B vitamins.

VITAMIN C. Vitamin C is synthesized by the dog and ascorbic acid deficiency is rare enough to be disregarded here.

VITAMIN D. Vitamin D is required in direct ratio to calcium and phosphorus for the formation of strong healthy bone. Lack of vitamin D produces rickets and subsequent other complications. Adequate vitamin D is very important during lactation. Fish liver oils and sunlight provide vitamin D.

VITAMIN E. Vitamin E helps assure healthy hearts, good reproduction and vigor. Unwilling breeders may suffer from lack of "E." Vitamin E deficiency in the mother has been linked to muscular dystrophy in puppies. Wheat germ and wheat germ oil are vital sources of vitamin E.

VITAMIN K. Vitamin K helps maintain regular blood clotting levels, and can be procured from fish meal, liver and green-leaf plants. "K" is synthesized by most animals. Excessive bleeding may indicate lack of vitamin K.

PROTEIN & CALCIUM. As a rule, both protein and calcium are present in commercial dog food products in the form of ground bone, which also provides phosphorus, copper, zinc, potassium, manganese, magnesium iron and iodine. Fish is another source of protein. When infection is not a factor, high mortality rate among new-born puppies can often be traced to insufficient protein in the mother's diet.

The exact interrelationship of vitamins and minerals within the metabolic processes has not been fully established, but without doubt, a significant imbalance can produce undesirable and often irreversible effects. Excessive overdosing with vitamins and minerals may have equally unfavorable side effects, and should be carefully avoided unless prescribed by a veterinarian.

ADDITIONAL SUPPLEMENTS. Linatone, a food supplement and skin and coat conditioner; Theralin Vitamin and Mineral Powder; Theralin V.M.P. tablets and Cal-D-Trons, raspberry flavored calcium tablets with D5 and phosphorus; and Avitron Vitamin Drops, are all highly recommended supplements by Lambert-Kay, and are readily available at your local pet center.

CHAPTER ELEVEN

THE OUTSIDE DOG

THERE ARE MANY commercial dog houses available, but dog owners who prefer to demonstrate their own ingenuity can convert old barrels, steel drums, packing cases, and numerous other items to advantage.

Personally I prefer an insulated wooden structure about five feet wide and three feet deep, just high enough for the dog to stand up in, with the actual sleeping area roughly three feet square, and the remaining two feet forming the entrance. The two areas are divided by a baffle, which helps to eliminate harmful drafts and also keeps the bedding in place. The roof is hinged so it can be lifted up for easy cleaning.

Cedar shavings are preferable as bedding, but clean straw will do in a pinch. Use about 50% less bedding in the summer time than during the rest of the year.

There are pros and cons about the merit of keeping dogs on a chain, as with keeping them confined in small pens. Neither alternative is totally satisfactory, yet each has its advantages. The main thing to remember is that the dog must be taken out for training and exercise every day. His existence must not be confined to a six foot by ten foot run, or to the amount of ground he can cover on the end of ten feet of chain.

A dog run should be at least six feet by ten feet, and about six feet high. The surface of the run can be made of packed dirt, concrete, patio blocks, black top or brick. The most popular surface is concrete, best when the slope on it is sufficient to allow for good drainage. Screened pea gravel, ¼ inch deep either by itself or mixed with black top, is a very good top layer and helps to tighten the dog's feet.

Black top has few advantages, for it gets hot and sticky in the summer and is not recommended unless the run is well shaded. Common red brick is preferable because it drains well, dries quickly, and is good for the feet.

An outside bedboard should be provided for the dog to lay on, and ample shade should be available during hot sunny weather.

Dogs kenneled outside should not be subjected to extreme changes in temperature, as may be experienced by taking them into an air-conditioned home in the summer, or into a heated house in the winter. Such abrupt changes are bad for them.

During very cold weather extra fat should be added to the diet—as indicated in the previous chapter. During hot spells, dogs are naturally inclined to eat less.

CHAPTER TWELVE

HIP DYSPLASIA AND SUBLUXATION

THE TERMS HIP dysplasia and subluxation refer to certain abnormal developments of the hip joint, such as a deformed femur or an enlargement or shallowing of the acetabulum that creates a loosely fitting joint. Varying degrees of lameness and immobility result, elaborately described in medical terminology as "a congenital predisposition to the malformation of the coxofemoral joint." The genetic factors governing the cause of this anomaly, which may be either unilateral or bilateral in effect, are exceedingly complex and have not, as yet, been fully determined.

Trauma, hematoma, septic inflammation and similar conditions, often resulting in pathological changes, have been identified in conjunction with the complaint. The syndrome prevails during the growing stages and may become progressively worse. Although congenital subluxation does not essentially immobilize a victim, secondary arthritic conditions may do so.

It has been established with some certainty that most affected individuals are the direct progeny of affected parents. Another disturbing feature is the fact that dysplasia is a known dominant, with irregular manifestations, so that only one defective gene is required, from either of the parents, to affect the offspring with certain qualified exceptions. For this reason, some schools of thought concerned with the abolition of this abnormality advocate extreme measures to prevent reproduction, such as castrating or spaying all affected animals. This alternative appears both impractical and ineffective inasmuch as it does not essentially eradicate the source.

The advisability of screening ALL prospective breeding stock, to insure a modicum of control, cannot be overstressed. Some time ago, Dr. Robert W. Bailey presented evidence that clinical examination is insufficient to determine dysplasia. He revealed that although all dogs donated to the Lakeland Air Force Sentry Dog Training Center were required to undergo physical examination by a civilian veterinarian before shipment, appoximately twenty percent of the X-rays taken after admittance showed varying degrees of this condition.

The relative degree of subluxation visible with radiographic technique may vary considerably according to the ability and experience of the operator. The diagnostic interpretation of X-rays is also a highly specialized field and not all veterinarians are qualified to render a conclusive opinion. As their signature on a certificate is apparently quite acceptable, it is important that all such documents are verified by a consultant radiologist.

Not all apparently weak or unsteady hindquarters are indicative of subluxation. Conversely, many powerfully proportioned and seemingly perfect specimens may be dysplastic. Dysplasia may also exist without subluxation. With insufficient data, statistics are impossible to compile, but it is estimated that a very high percentage of all puppies are born potentially dysplastic. Overweight puppies seem to be particularly susceptible, and a possible link here is being investigated.

Finding the solution to this complex and highly controversial problem constitutes a formidable challenge to breeders. Their most important step in the right direction has been to acknowledge that the problem exists, with much more serious consequences to follow, unless adequate preventive measures are taken before it is too late.

The presence of dysplasia is virtually impossible to detect in young puppies due to uncalcified epiphysis. However, perpetual lameness, front or rear; a marked reluctance to run or play for any length of time; wincing if touched on the hindquarters, especially around the hips; apparent looseness of the hip joint; staggering, with a tendency to fall to one side or favor one leg, should all alert the owner to the possibility of hip dysplasia. Subluxation (which is a slight dislocation) occurs following the erosion of either or both of the articulating surfaces.

All breeding stock should be X-rayed and certified by the Orthopedic Foundation for Animals. X-rays can be sent for certification to the Orthopedic Foundation for Animals, 817 Virginia Avenue, Columbia, Missouri 65201.

CHAPTER THIRTEEN

DOG SHOWS AND PROCEDURE

THERE ARE TWO basic types of Dog Shows conducted under the auspices of the American Kennel Club—Licensed Shows and Sanctioned Matches.

A Licensed Show is one in which championship points are awarded. A Sanctioned Match, although conducted along similar lines, is much more informal and carries no championship points.

Entries to a Licensed Show must be made on an Official American Kennel Club Entry Form, duly signed by the owner or authorized agent of the dog in question.

This form must be mailed to the Show Superintendent, and arrive before the closing date for entries at that show, generally two or three weeks before the actual show. The closing date and all other relevant details of entry requirements are listed in the Official Premium List.

Premium Lists can be obtained from the office of the show's superintendent. A list of forthcoming shows, along with the names of the superintendents, is published every month in *Pure-Bred Dogs*, The American Kennel Gazette. A single copy can be obtained for $1 by writing to 51 Madison Avenue, New York, N.Y. 10010.

A.K.C. LICENSED SHOWS. These are the regular classes for each breed variety: Puppy, Novice, Bred-by-Exhibitor, American-Bred, or Open.

OFFICIAL AMERICAN KENNEL CLUB ENTRY FORM

- - - INSERT BELOW — NAME OF CLUB and DATE OF SHOW - - -

CLUB

DATE

☛ **ENTRY FORM MUST BE SIGNED** on the bottom line ● by the owner or the owner's duly authorized agent, otherwise entry cannot be accepted.

MAKE CHECKS payable to Foley Dog Show Organization, Inc.

MAIL ENTRIES with FEES to Alan P. Winks, Superintendent, 2009 Ranstead Street, Philadelphia, Pa. 19103.

PLEASE TYPEWRITE OR PRINT CLEARLY

I ENCLOSE $_____ for entry fees.

● **IMPORTANT—Read Carefully Instructions on Reverse Side Before Filling Out**

Breed		Variety (if any) See Instruction #1, reverse side	Sex
	Dog Show Class	See Instruction #2, reverse side (Give age, color or weight if class divided)	**Obedience Trial Class**
	If dog is entered for Best of Breed (Variety) Competition —see Instruction #3 reverse side—CHECK THIS BOX. ☐		**Additional Classes**

Name of Actual Owner(s)	See Instruction #4, reverse side	
Name of Licensed Handler (if any)	(handler) ●	
Full Name of Dog		●
A.K.C. Reg. Number OR Litter Number	(OR I. L. P. Number) ILP	●
OR Foreign Reg. Number	(and country) ( ) ●	
Date of Birth	Check Place of Birth (Do not print in catalog) ☐ U.S.A. ☐ Canada ☐ Foreign	●
	Breeder,	● By
Sire		—
Dam		●

Owner's Address — Street _____

City _____ State _____ Zip Code _____

I CERTIFY that I am the actual owner of this dog, or that I am the duly authorized agent of the actual owner whose name I have entered above. In consideration of the acceptance of this entry, I (we) agree to abide by the rules and regulations of The American Kennel Club in effect at the time of this show or obedience trial, and by any additional rules and regulations appearing in the premium list for this show or obedience trial or both, and further agree to be bound by the "Agreement" printed on the reverse side of this entry form. I (we) certify and represent that the dog entered is **not a hazard to persons or other dogs.** This entry is submitted for acceptance on the foregoing representation and agreement.

SIGNATURE of owner or his agent ●
duly authorized to make this entry _____

Puppy Classes may be in two divisions, one for puppies six to nine months, and another for those nine to twelve months. A puppy cannot be entered at a points show if he is under six months of age on the day the show opens. Puppies become adult at one year of age.

The *Novice Class* is for dogs over six months old that have not won three first prizes in that class nor a first prize in any of the other regular classes other than the Puppy Class. Only dogs whelped in the United States or Canada can compete in the Novice Class.

The *Bred-by-Exhibitor Class* is for dogs, except champions, which are owned or co-owned by the breeder, and are shown by the breeder, or any member of his immediate family.

The *American-Bred Class* is for all dogs, except champions, whelped in the United States by reason of a breeding that took place in this country.

The *Open Class* is for any dog six months of age or older. Foreign bred dogs, except Canadian bred, must compete in this class, until they become champions.

The *Winners Class* for males is held after the judging of all the regular classes of that sex has been completed. Each blue ribbon winner is entitled to enter this class, provided he has not been beaten in any of the other classes. The dog placing first in the Winners Class is awarded Champion Points, if the size of the entry meets the necessary requirements. The dog beaten only by the winner of the Winners Class is then allowed to compete with the remaining class winners for Reserve Winners. This is an important award because in the event that the Winners Dog is disqualified, for any reason whatsoever, the Reserve Winner then becomes the Points Winner. The whole procedure is repeated in the Bitch classes.

Best of Breed Competition brings together the Winners Dog and Winners Bitch, to compete with any champions that may be entered in inter-sex competition. In addition to the purple and gold ribbon, the Best of Breed, or Variety Winner receives the distinction of representing its particular breed in the Group Competition later in the show. (If no champions are entered, then Best of Winners is automatically Best of Breed.)

Best of Winners is then selected between the Winners Dog and Winners Bitch. If one of the two was previously selected Best of Breed, or Variety, it would automatically become Best of Winners. The Best of Winners is entitled to receive the maximum number of points awarded that day, proportionate to the entry in the regular classes of each individual breed. For example, if the Winners Dog wins two points, and the Winners Bitch wins three points (or more), and the Winners Dog goes Best of Winners, he would also receive the same number of points as the Winners Bitch. This would not detract any points from the Winners Bitch.

Best of Opposite Sex is the final selection in breed competition. A dog or bitch, whichever is of the opposite sex to the Best of Breed or Variety winner, is selected as Best of Opposite Sex from among the eligible competitors.

Group Judging takes place after all the breeds in that group have been judged and a Best of Breed or Variety has been selected for each breed or variety. The German Shepherd belongs to the Working Group, which represents 30 breeds. The other groups are Hounds, Terrier, Toy, Sporting and Non-Sporting.

Lastly, the winner of each respective group competes for the most important award of all—*Best in Show*.

To become an A.K.C. Champion of Record, a dog must win a total of fifteen Championship points at A.K.C. Licensed Shows, under three different judges. These points must include at least two "Majors." A Major consists of three, four or five points won at a single show. In order to win a three-point

Major in the northern and eastern areas of the country, a German Shepherd must beat a total of 34 dogs or 37 bitches in regular class competition, or win a Working Group, or Best in Show, where there was a Major entry.

The points schedule is revised annually and is based on the number of German Shepherds registered in that area the previous year. This scale will vary in different parts of the country. A complete American Kennel Club Schedule of Points is published in every Dog Show Catalog and is revised annually.

SANCTIONED MATCHES. These matches are judged in the same way as Licensed Shows, but, as no points are awarded, the Winners and Best of Winners Classes are eliminated. Instead, the bitch classes follow straight on after the dog classes. Then all unbeaten males and females compete in intersex competition to determine Best of Breed. Champions cannot be shown at Sanction Matches. Classes for puppies under six months of age are usually scheduled at these shows.

Entries to a Sanctioned Match need not be mailed in advance, but can be made at the show grounds on the day of the show. For information about Sanctioned Matches in your area, contact the secretary of your local All Breed or Obedience Club.

CHAPTER FOURTEEN

GROOMING

IF YOUR DOG is in good condition, only minimal grooming should be required before he is ready for the ring. An outside dog may require an occasional bath, which can either be done at home or at a grooming shop. If you intend to give him the bath yourself, either bathe the dog in your own bathtub or use a bucket and hose in the back yard. In either case, sponge him down well with "Johnson's Baby Shampoo" and rinse him thoroughly. Make sure that no soap remains in the undercoat.

Towel dry your dog and put him in his crate to dry. After he is dry, give him a good brushing and combing. A fine comb is preferable as it will strip out any surplus undercoat that could otherwise show through his outer coat.

Trim his nails short and clean out his ears. Cut off his whiskers and other long hairs on his head. Trim the long hair from around and under the feet. With a pair of thinning shears, trim the long hair from the underside of the tail so that it looks slightly flat. Trim the straggly hairs around the sides of the neck and under his body so that he presents a neat outline. Spray on a little "Pro-Groom" coat dressing and brush his coat until it has a deep-down shine.

A Shepherd is not at his most attractive if he is too barbered, so don't overdo the trimming until you have had a chance to see how the experts do it!

CHAPTER FIFTEEN

THE PROFESSIONAL HANDLER

SOME OWNERS WOULD like to show their dogs but lack the time or perhaps the ability to do it themselves. Such a person should seriously consider using the specialized services of a professional dog handler.

A professional handler is a person annually licensed by the American Kennel Club to exhibit dogs at A.K.C. Licensed Shows for a fee. This fee usually varies with the amount of work done in conjunction with handling the dog, such as boarding, grooming and transportation. Extra "bonuses" may also be charged for winning Championship points, Best of Breed, Group placements, or Best in Show.

All fees and additional charges should be clearly understood before entering into any form of agreement with a handler.

To the novice, the cost of professional handling may appear to be expensive, but it frequently works out to be cheaper than showing the dog yourself, because of the handler's professional skill and superior knowledge of the breed.

CHAPTER SIXTEEN

BREEDING

EXCEPT FOR THE occasional "nymphomaniac," a condition due to cystic ovaries, bitches will only mate during certain times of the year which coincide with ovulation. This period is commonly known as a "heat."

The start of the heat is indicated by a "show of color"— a bloody discharge from the vagina—usually accompanied by a noticeable swelling of the vulva. Subtle personality or behavior changes may precede this discharge, such as continual licking of the external organs, irritability, snappiness, or disobedience. A bitch may start frequently wetting or "spotting," sometimes against a post or a tree, to advertise her whereabouts and availability to all the males in the neighborhood when she becomes ready to breed.

A normal heat can be expected to last up to twenty-one days, and precautions must be taken to ensure that the female remains isolated from all males during that entire time. Bitches first come into heat at about nine months of age, but this time may easily vary anywhere between six and fifteen months, even among litter mates. However, it has frequently been observed that most bitches in the same kennel "come in" either together, or within a short time of each other.

After the initial heat, which may vary both in length and intensity, depending on the age of the individual, a bitch will usually come into heat again approximately every six months. A few bitches only have one heat per year.

Under normal circumstances it is not considered good practice to mate a female before her second heat unless she is over twelve months of age.

If you are planning to breed your bitch for the first time, your most important consideration should be the choice of a stud dog. Your preference should be based on several important points—namely, the quality of the puppies that you are hoping to produce, the amount of the stud fee that you are prepared to pay, and the availability of the stud in question.

Hopefully, anyone who considers himself a serious fancier of a breed will hope to effect some improvement in each coming generation. On that premise, you should choose the best available stud that you can comfortably afford. If preparations are made in good time, you can ship your bitch either by Air or Railway Express to most parts of the country, although accompanying her yourself is usually the most satisfying.

The mating should take place about ten to fifteen days after the first show of color. A simple ovulation test can be performed by inserting a strip of "Tes-Tape" into the vagina. Tes-Tape is a urine sugar analysis paper, generally used by diabetics, and is available from any drug store. During the critical ovulation period, a bitch secretes an abnormally high concentration of sugar in the vagina that is not present at other times. Its presence is indicated by the Tes-Tape turning bright green in color. Sometimes just a few green spots will appear, but any green staining that indicates a ¼ % concentration or more should be considered positive for breeding.

The mating procedure is usually left to the owner of the stud. Some very good studs may refuse to work in the presence of strangers. The female may require restraining at first, which should also be left to the discretion of the owner of the stud. The owner of the bitch may not like the idea of having his bitch muzzled for the occasion, but even very placid females have been known to inflict severe bites on their would-be suitors.

Some stud owners like to breed twice, a day apart, while

others allow only one mating. The stud fee, which is considered payment for the use of the dog and not for producing puppies, is payable at the time of service and is not refundable. Most stud owners, however, will grant you the courtesy of a free return service if the bitch should miss. A breeding is presumed to have taken place when the pair have had a satisfactory "tie" of at least several minutes.

Following the tie, the female should be confined to her crate and not be allowed to run around for at least thirty minutes. Nor should she be allowed to come into contact with other males until at least 20 days after the first show of color. It is quite possible for a female to be successfully bred by two different males and for her to produce puppies by both of them.

After the breeding has taken place, give your bitch "No-Mate" tablets to discourage the attention of unwanted suitors.

If your bitch is accidentally bred by an undesirable male, either before or after she has been bred to the stud of your choice, consult your vet right away. An injection of Estradiol, or a daily oral administration of Diethylstilbestrol for five days, will usually recycle the heat. This eliminates the possibility of an unwanted litter. It is not considered good practice to re-mate a bitch following this treatment, although there is no objection to breeding her during her next normal heat period.

BREEDING THE MALE. Sooner or later, most new dog owners desire to breed their male, frequently because they would like to have a puppy sired by him. Other owners are drawn to the idea because it is an easy way to make a few extra dollars. Some owners even feel that they owe it to the dog because he's such a nice pet! All three reasons are of dubious merit. Moreover, an attempt by inexperienced owners to breed two equally inexperienced dogs often turns into a fantastic comedy of errors.

The most frequent mistake is to take the male to visit the bitch, which takes him out of his territorial domain, and in most cases makes him feel and act insecure. Conversely, the bitch is right at home, and often is ready to tear the "intruder" apart—without consideration for his amorous intentions. The first rule is always bring *her* to *him*.

The second most common mistake is to allow the two dogs to romp around together, either in an enclosed yard or in the garage or basement until both are exhausted. In addition, the female has the opportunity to turn on the dog whenever he attempts to mate her, thus intimidating him, despite the fact that she might have seemed very amenable at their initial introduction.

Always restrain the female, for bitches in heat are very unpredictable. Always tie her muzzle loosely with a length of bandage before the two are brought together. Have someone hold the bitch's head and try to keep her still. Sometimes her owner can do that if the male does not object, but otherwise, use someone the dog knows.

Allow the male to briefly sniff the bitch and lick her ear if he is so inclined. Encourage him to mount by patting the female on the rump while giving him a few coaxing words. Of course, if you discouraged him when, as a pup, he demonstrated his developing sex instincts, it's quite possible that he won't believe that you have had a sudden change of heart.

Once the minor problems have been overcome and the pair are "tied" (the male swells up after insertion and the two cannot separate until the breeding is over), the male must be "turned." To do this, gently lift his front legs onto the ground on one side of the bitch. Then, take hold of his rear legs on the opposite side and carefully raise them over the bitch's back so that they are standing back to back. Be careful to move the tails up out of the way at the same time.

The tie will last anywhere from five minutes to over an hour. The average tie is fifteen minutes in duration. During that time the dogs should not be left unattended as they might try to pull away from each other and could easily be injured.

CHAPTER SEVENTEEN

WHELPING AND AFTERCARE

AFTER BEING BRED, the female requires little more than routine care. Prenatal Theralin should be added to the food to provide extra minerals and vitamins. She should be allowed to exercise in normal fashion, although excessive jumping or running up and down stairs is not recommended. After the first six weeks, the amount of food she eats should be increased slightly and divided into two meals a day. A bitch in whelp should be in good condition but not be allowed to become overweight. If the bitch is very overweight when she is bred, her normal rations should be reduced. Specialized Pet Diet #3 (for controlling obesity) is specially formulated for "normalizing" overweight dogs.

Although the normal gestation period is 63 days, a great majority of bitches produce two or three days early. For this reason your expectant mother should be given her whelping box at least one week before she is due. The whelping box can be as simple or as elaborate as you choose to make it.

My personal preference is for a large, fairly deep, heavy-duty cardboard box (easily found at the back of any supermarket or appliance center), lined with newspapers, and big enough for the bitch to stretch out in. A small door should be cut out of one side to allow the bitch to get in and out without jumping over the edge. This type of whelping box is easily changed when it becomes soiled, and does not have to be stored after the puppies have been reared.

When her time is due, the bitch will usually become restless, scratching up her newspaper and often tearing it with her teeth. She may pant heavily or tremble and appear noticeably distressed. At this point it is advisable to check her temperature, using a lubricated blunt nose rectal thermometer. If her temperature has dropped one or two degrees below the normal 101.4°, whelping time should not be far away. Once the contractions start, it should not be too long before the puppies start to arrive. If heavy contractions go on for too long, or subside without results, your veterinarian should be consulted. Complicated births may require his expert attention.

There are numerous problems that might occur during whelping, especially with a maiden bitch. Of these, "uterine inertia" is undoubtedly the most common, a term referring to either the inability or unwillingness on the part of the bitch to continue normal labor contractions, caused either by fear of the pain or by exhaustion. The normal veterinary procedure in such cases is to give the bitch an injection of one of the various oxytoxic agents designed to accelerate labor. However, in cases where fear is the prime inhibiting factor, a few tablespoons of brandy diluted in warm water often produces the required results.

Breech presentations, where the puppy arrives backward, i.e., feet first, occur quite frequently. Generally this does not present too much of a problem unless either one or both of the hind legs get hung up. These can be freed by careful manipulation.

In some cases, the head may be exceptionally large and the whelp will be partly out but appear stuck. In such instances, the bitch may get up and run around with the whelp hanging from her. First of all, make her lie down. Then, with a hand-towel wrapped around the exposed portion of the whelp, gently withdraw it in a slightly downward direction, away from the bitch's tail. Try to coordinate your pull with the contractions. Steady controlled traction should always be used. Never tug or jerk when trying to remove either the whelp or the placenta. A surprising amount of force can be exerted without injury to the whelp, but this consideration should be secondary. The bitch may yelp as the puppy comes free, which is only to be expected. To remove the afterbirth, grasp the cord close to the bitch, preferably with a pair of forceps, and gently draw it away.

In any event, if the bitch fails to produce after two hours of prolonged labor, call your veterinarian.

The main point to remember is not to panic. Whelping is a normal process and the majority of bitches will instinctively know how to take care of themselves.

The indication of the impending arrival of a puppy is the appearance of the chorian, a membranous sac containing the puppy and filled with the amniotic fluid which surrounds the embryo in the womb. As a rule, the mother is quick to tear the sac and free the puppy. This is followed by vigorous licking, which stimulates the puppy into immediate activity as well as drying it off. The mother will usually sever the umbilical cord and then eat the placenta, or afterbirth. The contents of the placenta are highly nutritious and if the bitch eats them willingly, she should not be discouraged from doing so.

If by chance she should appear hesitant to take care of the newborn, you may assist by tearing the membrane apart with your fingers. You can also cut the umbilical cord with a pair of dull scissors. Before doing so, tie off the cord with some strong thread about an inch from the puppy's stomach to prevent needless loss of blood.

If a puppy does not start to breathe as soon as it is released, rub it vigorously in a towel between your hands. Keep its head down as you do this in order to expel any fluid that might have entered the lungs. Artificial respiration can also be given by opening the puppy's mouth and breathing into it, followed immediately by applying pressure with your cupped hands on either side of its ribcage. Do this before cutting the umbilical cord.

After each puppy has been born and preliminaries are taken

care of, it should be encouraged to nurse. While most puppies are both willing and anxious to do so, if one appears to be sluggish, attach it to a convenient easy-to-nurse nipple.

Sometimes a maiden bitch will be afraid of her newborn whelps. If the bitch is made to lie on her side and nurse her puppies, by forceable restraint if necessary, she will eventually settle down to her duties without undue fussing.

As each puppy is born, the paper around the mother will get wet and messy, and must be changed. If you start off with numerous sheets of newspaper, it is a simple matter to slip the soiled ones away without unduly disturbing the family. If the litter is very large, remove the early arrivals and put them in a cardboard box where they will be warm, leaving only one or two of the more recent arrivals with the mother.

Once the whelping is over, the bitch should be offered a drink of water and perhaps a little food, although she will probably not want to eat for the next twelve to twenty-four hours. This is normal and should not be taken as an indication that something is wrong. Whether or not she eats or drinks, the bitch must be put out to exercise for a few minutes at regular intervals. This will also provide you with the opportunity of cleaning up the whelping box and checking out the puppies. Overhandling the whelps is inadvisable during the early stages and should be kept to a minimum.

To ensure that each of the newborn whelps is receiving sufficient fluid from the mother, they should be individually tested for any sign of dehydration at regular intervals for the first few days. Gently pinch the loose skin on the back of the puppy's neck, just above the shoulders, using your index finger and thumb. If the puppy is in normal condition, the skin will be quite elastic and quick to return to its normal position. However, if the puppy has not been getting enough fluid intake, the skin loses its resiliency and remains puckered up.

Dehydration can be treated by giving supplementary amounts of dextrose or glucose solution with an eyedropper. A suitable solution can be made by dissolving a tablespoon of dextrose or glucose in eight ounces of boiled (but not boiling) water. Allow the solution to cool to blood temperature (98 to 100 degrees) before giving it in small quantities to the puppy. An eyedropperful, given every two hours, should be sufficient. If the treatment is successful, the puppy's skin will return to its normal resiliency.

If the mother does not have enough milk to feed her litter, Borden's "Esbilac," a bitches' milk substitute, may be used to supplement the dam's supply. For the best results, follow the directions on the Esbilac label.

There are two basic ways to give the formula to large puppies: either by using a regular baby nurser, or by injecting the fluid directly into the stomach with a tube attached to a syringe. The latter method is quicker by far and takes only minutes to learn. A complete tube feeding kit with detailed instructions can be obtained from Kay-9 Specialties, 31759 Florida Street, Redlands, California 92373.

A whelp that is reared in the nest is constantly being licked and rolled around by its mother, which serves to stimulate its normal body functions. When a puppy is taken away from its mother at a very early age, it is essential to provide a substitute for this action in order to regulate the bowels. With a piece of cotton or tissue that has been soaked in warm water and then squeezed out until just damp, wipe the puppy's stomach between its hind legs and under its tail after each feeding to make it urinate and defecate. If the puppy is restless, then apply a dab of Vaseline to the area to prevent chapping.

If you are hand-rearing a whole litter, keep all the whelps in small separate compartments. Otherwise, they will be inclined to suck on each other, with obviously undesirable results. To keep the youngsters warm, a small heating pad on low heat, wrapped in a towel under a few sheets of newspaper, works very well.

Puppies that are doing well will remain quiet and contented. If whelps are noisy and restless, then something is wrong with them. This rule applies whether they are being reared by hand or by the mother. If they are unsettled, investigate to discover the problem, for crying is the only way puppies show that they are uncomfortable.

For those interested in establishing their own line, remember that hand-reared females rarely make good mothers. They apparently fail to develop normal maternal instincts unless they themselves are reared naturally.

ECLAMPSIA. This is a disease that occurs to the bitch after whelping, as the result of insufficient calcium. Symptoms may appear any time after whelping but usually occur within the first two weeks, especially if the dam is nursing a very large litter.

At first the bitch may become nervous and restless, and may also cry and whine a lot. Her legs may get stiff and she may become unsteady on her feet. Her temperature may jump as high as 107 degrees. This is followed by collapse and convulsions in which the neck and legs are rigidly extended, then by periods of relaxation or twitching, then by more convulsions.

A bitch with eclampsia must be taken to a veterinarian immediately for an injection of calcium gluconate and possible sedation. Recovery is rapid and usually highly dramatic.

Eclampsia can be avoided by giving the pregnant bitch calcium-vitamin-mineral supplements such as Prenatal Theralin and Cal-D-Trons tablets.

Puppies belonging to a bitch that has had eclampsia are often prone to develop rickets and should be started on calcium supplements as soon as possible.

Always keep a written record of each litter for future reference. A simple chart, similar to the one shown below, will help you to do just that, with a minimum of effort.

Sire	Dam	Date Bred	Date Due	Date Whelped	Number	Weight	Pups Weaned	Pups Wormed	Shots	Pups Sold	
										Age	Date

CHAPTER EIGHTEEN

COMMON AILMENTS

ANAL GLANDS. The anal sacs are located between the internal and external sphincter muscles, on either side of the lower portion of the anus. The specific function of the organ remains undetermined, but a recent theory suggests that it may serve as a means of protection for the weaker and older animals. In moments of extreme fear, involuntary elimination of the anal sacs occurs. This results in a pungent odor unpleasant to humans that surprisingly affects male dogs in an identical manner to a bitch in season. So, if an old or weak male is attacked by a stronger aggressor, the discharge of this secretion serves to distract the aggressor.

Incorrectly expressing the anal sacs can cause an abscess, but occasionally they become impacted, creating discomfort to the dog, and must be treated. This procedure is rather distasteful to the average person and is best left to your veterinarian.

BAD BREATH (HALITOSIS). This is often caused by tartar or bad teeth. Another cause can be digestive upset due to poor diet. Chewing hard biscuits, such as "Milk-Bone," helps to prevent tartar build-up.

It is necessary to clean dogs' teeth more frequently today than in the past, one reason being the modern method of feeding. While traditional dog bones might help to keep the teeth strong and clean, they can also perforate the intestine.

Many generations of well-meaning owners have failed to realize that a dog in its wild state did NOT eat just bones. He ate other animals, including hair and intestines, which acted as padding for splintered bone fragments.

Periodically cleaning the teeth with peroxide helps to remove organic material. Small tartar deposits can be removed by scraping with the milled edge of a small coin. Further buildup can be prevented by occasionally rubbing the stained areas on the teeth with a damp cotton swab dipped in a small amount of kitchen cleanser. If the dog's gums are inflamed, or the teeth are loose or have cavities and require extraction, call your veterinarian. Gastric problems usually respond to a suitable change of diet. In the case of older dogs, Specialized Pet Diet #1 (for aging dogs) may prove beneficial.

BITES. Minor bites usually heal without problems, but deep bites frequently become badly infected because the surface of the wound tends to heal over before the lesion has had a chance to granulate. An abscess is then formed that, if untreated, could develop into a major source of infection. In addition to a thorough cleansing of the wound, antibiotic treatment, in the form of a long-lasting shot of penicillin, is generally indicated.

CASTRATION. Castration is not recommended as an instant cure for normal male behavior, and should be undertaken only for sound pathological reasons.

COCCIDIOSIS. There are four types of coccidia known to affect dogs, puppies being particularly susceptible. Infected animals suffer first from diarrhea, which soon develops into dysentery. The feces contain blood and mucus. Dehydration accompanied by general disability will result. If untreated, puppies may develop a cough or slight fever with runny eyes and nose, go into convulsions, and die. A few make spontaneous recovery.

Coccidiosis results from a filthy contaminatéd environment and is often accompanied by the more serious infections also associated with such conditions.

Treatment may vary, but coccidiosis usually responds favorably to sulforamide drugs. Occasionally, all treatments fail. The best safeguards against coccidiosis, and most other diseases, are sanitary living conditions and good management practice.

CONSTIPATION. This can result from a poor diet or allowing the dog to eat bones, often coupled with insufficient exercise. Mineral oil can be given to relieve the problem, but in bad cases an enema may be necessary, after which time the dog should be kept on a more suitable diet.

DIARRHEA. Dogs, especially puppies, may develop violent diarrhea for no immediately apparent reason. Parasites, poisoning, infection, excitement, heat, overfeeding, change of diet or diet deficiency, raw meat (especially liver), fat, and lactose in cows' milk are among the more frequent causes of diarrhea. The younger the dog is, the more easily affected he will be.

While the problem has to be remedied at the source, the initial requirement is to treat the symptom. Apart from being messy to give, "Kaopectate" is effective and generally available in an emergency, although "Pet Pectillin" usually provides the most prompt relief. Food should be withheld initially, but water should remain available. A bland diet such as Specialized Pet Diet #4 (Intestinal Diet) may also help to stabilize minor gastric disorders. Never give laxatives in cases of diarrhea.

Unless you are reasonably certain that the diarrhea does not stem from one of the more serious causes, consult your veterinarian. Remember that diarrhea is not a sickness, but rather a symptom.

EARS. Ears should be cleaned regularly as a hygienic precaution, and to remove wax and debris from inside the ear. Using "Ear-Rite" twice a month will help to reduce ear problems.

EYES. Eyes should be checked at frequent intervals. "Eye-Brite," a mild astringent solution, helps to soothe and clear up minor irritations.

HEATSTROKE. Heatstroke can occur during very hot weather, or when a dog (especially a black one) is kept out too long in the hot sun. Its onset is characterized by sudden collapse, accompanied by abnormally rapid or deep breathing. The dog may choke or vomit and develop a staring expression. Death is not uncommon when treatment is delayed. Carry the dog into the shade and splash cold water all over him. Apply an ice pack or wet cloth to the head or cover the dog with a wet towel. Give him a limited amount of cool water to drink, and make him rest quietly in a cool place.

INJURY & SHOCK. Almost any type of accident which results in physical injury or pain can induce a state of shock. The blood pressure drops and the pulse becomes rapid and weak. The gums become pale, almost gray in color. The dog might be in a state of collapse or very quiet. His eyes may appear sunken or staring. Breathing may be shallow with occasional sharp gasps. A dog that has been injured and is in shock should be kept warm and quiet and transported to a veterinary hospital as quickly as possible.

Broken limbs must be gently supported while an injured dog is being moved. Bleeding from any of the external orifices indicates internal injury. Some attempt should be made to stem the loss of blood from open wounds, either by applying steady pressure to the area or by the use of a bandage, which should not be applied so tightly that the circulation stops.

For open wounds on the legs or tail, a tourniquet may be applied, but must be released every ten to fifteen minutes to restore circulation. Do not give the dog anything by mouth without first consulting your veterinarian.

ITCHING. If your dog keeps itching and scratching, but does not have fleas or ticks, try "Itch Free Emulsion," a product guaranteed to stop itching and scratching. A topical application of "Cortisynth" ointment will often help clear up minor skin irritations.

KENNEL COUGH. Coughing due to minor throat irritation can be controlled with "Resta-Kof," a non-narcotic cough suppressor for dogs.

NAILS. Nails must always be kept short, as long nails will make dogs' feet spread. The "Twinco" nail trimmer is easy to use and comes complete with instructions. If you should happen to cut the quick and make the nail bleed, do not worry. A little "Blood-Stop" or ferric subsulfate (from the drugstore) forced into the cut nail will soon take care of the problem.

OVERWEIGHT. Overweight dogs can benefit from Specialized Pet Diet #3 (obesity diet) which provides a low energy, low fat diet to aid the consumption of excess body fat while the body maintains normal energy levels. It also has a high nutritive value to maintain the vital organic functions.

RINGWORM. In most animals and in humans, ringworm is characterized by round or semi-round hairless lesions. Strangely enough, cats may carry this infection without such indication. A "country cure" is to hold a fairly large lump of ice in firm contact with the infected area for a full ten minutes. This unorthodox treatment really works. If you suspect ringworm, have your veterinarian check for fungus with a Wood's Lamp. In the event of infection, he will no doubt prescribe something more scientific, such as Griseofulvin.

SKUNK ODOR. Rub the "sprayed" area with tomato juice, leave it on the coat for at least fifteen minutes, and then rinse it off. Repeat if necessary, and let the dog dry out in the sun. If you are in an area where skunks are common, it might pay to keep a package of "Odormute" on hand, a non-toxic enzyme product that will help control animal odor. Odormute's advertised function is to control odor in dog runs, etc. For skunk odor, use one tablespoonful to a gallon of water, allow the solution to remain on the coat for thirty minutes, and then rinse off.

As 1,400 cases of rabies were reported among skunks in 1968, the highest number of any animal, it would seem a good idea to keep your dog away from them.

SPAYING. Spaying (Ovarichysterectomy) is the surgical removal of the ovaries and the uterus. Spaying is the obvious answer to the problem associated with the "heat," when you do not intend to breed from a bitch. Most veterinarians recommend that a female should not be spayed until after she has had at least one normal heat.

STINGS. Stings can usually be attributed either to bees or wasps. It is a simple matter to distinguish between the two as the bee always leaves its sting behind. First remove the sting, then apply alkaline (such as a slice of raw potato) to neutralize its effect. A wasp sting requires acid to neutralize it, and vinegar or lemon juice will usually work. In the event of a bad allergic reaction, a "Contac" capsule can be given as an emergency measure.

TATTOO. As protection against dog-napping, you can have your dog's A.K.C. registration number tattooed on the inside of his flank as a means of permanent identification.

However, the Canine Bureau of Identification suggests that you use your telephone number for a tattoo.

UNDERWEIGHT. Underweight dogs can be given "Stim-U-Wate," a high calorie food supplement which aids in stimulating the appetite and helps the dog to put on weight.

CHAPTER NINETEEN

THINGS TO REMEMBER

DO   check out the puppy after the children have been playing with him. Look for elastic bands or bits of string that might be cutting off the circulation, especially around the neck, muzzle, ears, tail, and legs.

DO   check his collar regularly if he wears one all the time and let it out as necessary. There have been many incidents where collars have been left on so tightly that they have eaten deep into the flesh, causing untold misery.

DO   check your puppy for ticks after a romp in the woods. Check under his "arm pits" between his rear legs, under his feet and between his toes for painful burrs. A good way to remove burrs is with a fork.

DO   check your puppy's rear-end to see that it does not get encrusted and dirty.

DO   train your puppy. A dog left to its own devices usually makes a poor pet.

DO   brush your dog at least once a week.

DON'T   carry puppies around, but let them walk, for puppies need exercise. Besides, why should a person with only two legs carry around a dog which has four legs!

DON'T   take good behavior for granted. Praise your dog when he does the right thing, but always correct him if he is wrong. Remember, time makes puppies older, not necessarily better behaved.

DON'T   fuss with the puppy all the time, for he becomes tired of it. Save the fussing for special occasions and he will appreciate it more.

DON'T   give puppies round-steak bones, thinking that the puppies cannot eat them. The bones sometimes slip over the dog's lower jaws, becoming lodged behind the canine teeth in such a fashion that a veterinarian is required to remove them.

DON'T   leave your dog or puppy locked up in your auto with the windows closed, except perhaps during the winter. Hundreds of dogs are suffocated annually in locked autos. On a hot sunny day, leave your dog at home. If you must have him with you, try to park in the shade as much as possible, leave the windows partly open, and check periodically to see that the dog is not distressed. NEVER put a dog in the trunk of a car.

DON'T   let your dog annoy others, for not everyone likes dogs. Respect another person's outlook.

DON'T   leave your dog, especially a black one, chained out in the hot sun. Many dogs die each year from being left out without any shade.

DON'T   let your dog run wild. The maximum danger of infection exists among uncontrolled strays, as well as the possibility of injury on the highway.

DON'T   let flies eat your dog alive. They can cause painful injury to your pet, especially to the ears. If your dog is exposed to flies, use "Flies-Off" or "Ticks-Off" on all exposed areas.